Prague in Legends

ILLUSTRATIONS BY
JAN KLIMEŠ

PRÁH

The book was published
with the support of the City of Prague.

ISBN 978-80-7252-618-5

Prague in Legends

ILLUSTRATIONS BY
JAN KLIMEŠ

PRÁH

Prague

Long ago the Czechs were ruled by the wise Princess Libuše, a noble and clement woman, both just and resolute. All the people respected her for her prophetic abilities, through which she could predict the distant future.

One day, as she was standing on the rock at Vyšehrad looking down towards the Vltava River at the places where Prague stretches out today, before her eyes the dark forests parted and the trees began to take on the form of houses, palaces and high-towered cathedrals. Overcome by the vision, Libuše proclaimed these famous words:

"I see a great city whose glory shall reach the stars! If it is the will of the gods, so be it. Thus shall I myself lay the foundation of this city and let it grow and flourish to the glory of my line and future times."

The next day Libuše sent out servants to find the best place to found the city, and she ordered them:

"Take heed: if you see anyone performing any kind of work in these places, I shall name the future city after it!"

The men came to the plain beneath what is today Petřín Hill and it seemed to them suitable for founding a city. There they came across two men who were hewing a thick tree trunk.

"What are you doing here?" they asked.

"We are carving a threshold," the carpenters responded.

The men returned to the rock at Vyšehrad and recounted to the princess what they had seen.

"Then at that place I shall found a city," Libuše responded, "about whose future glory I have no doubt. And I shall name it Prague (*Praha*) after the threshold (*prah*) that the men were carving there."

And so it was. And none of the later rulers ever dared to change that name.

Prague Castle

ŽITO THE MAGICIAN

The popularity of jesters and magicians at royal courts is nothing unusual. They entertain the noble courtiers and amuse them to help pass the time. Such is the rule.

King Wenceslas IV became very fond of a magician called Žito, a great master of his trade. He was inscrutable, particularly in transformations. One day he would turn up as the richest nobleman, another as the poorest pauper. Before the eyes of the court he could transform from a dirty gardener into a splendidly dressed wealthy merchant, then right into an urban dandy, only to leave the amazed nobles as a pilgrim in monk's robes.

The other royal jesters feared Žito, as he liked to punish any boastfulness with ridiculous transformations. Yet the way he responded to the bravado of the Bavarian Duke's magicians, that was unexpected. At first it appeared that Žito had nothing up his sleeve that the Bavarians could not repeat back to him, and it seemed that Žito would be defeated in this battle of magicians.

The time came for lunch and the foreigners sat down at the table and, pleased with themselves, began to feast. Suddenly from outside the windows of the banquet room, from the ground in front of the stage where the magic competition was to continue, a loud argument broke out. The Bavarian magicians, curious to know what was going on, rose from their meal and leant out of the window. Seeing nothing out of the ordinary they decided to return to the rich feast, when suddenly… Huh? What the...? Whatever they did they couldn't get their heads back in; they were stuck in the window frame. And no wonder! It was Žito's masterpiece – he had made large sets of antlers sprout on their heads. And the people in the courtyard laughed until their sides split.

There was one special feat that Prague spoke about for a long time. Žito set his sights on a miserly baker who cheated and stole from people wherever he could.

The baker had a herd of pigs that he took very good care of, regularly taking them to wallow in the mud of the Vltava wetlands. Once, Žito also herded his pigs there – all pink and plump. The baker couldn't take his eyes off them. His mouth watered with envy and when he could take no more he approached Žito:

"I say, Žito, what a nice herd you have. One piggy more beautiful than the next, all rosy and plump. I would like to buy them from you. For a decent price."

"They're not for sale," said Žito dismissively.

The baker pressed, and Žito danced about and stretched the baker out as if on a rack until they finally struck a bargain.

Žito then warned the baker: "The pigs are very well-fed, as you have noticed, but they do not like water. If you let them go in it, then you can say good-bye to them."

The baker had no sooner finished listening to Žito than he herded them toward his own team, which was wallowing in the mud by the Vltava. The pigs ran into the river, the water closed over them and sheaves of straw floated up to the surface... the sheaves that Žito had enchanted into the plump little pigs.

"Dear Lord, where have you gone? Help! My herd of thirty pigs is drowning! You there, fishermen! Fish them out!" called out the horrified baker, who had not yet realised that Žito had pulled a fast one on him. But when the fishermen kept pulling out sheaves of wet straw instead of pigs, he put two and two together and set off like a madman after the magician. He looked for him high and low until he found him in a pub in Malá Strana.

Žito was enjoying the money he had earned. He had already drunk a fair bit and was just lounging about, sprawled out, at the pub table. The baker was beside himself with fury. When he saw Žito he grabbed his leg and wanted to pull him onto the floor… but… oh, the horror!… the whole leg came off in his hand. Žito roared in pain and the whole pub turned on the baker:

"You thieving snake! You miserly miser! Fork over damages right now, you no-good snollygoster…"

The horrified and frightened baker dished out another pouch of gold to Žito, who then jumped up fit as a fiddle and before the eyes of the astonished patrons left the pub – on his own two legs.

Žito performed more tricks of this kind than one could count, but one day his art had to come to an end. That was the day that the Devil himself turned up, to whom Žito had sold his soul so as to learn all his wondrous magic. The Devil picked up his reward and carried it off to the place from where is no return.

DALIBOR AND DALIBORKA

One of the towers of Prague Castle, Daliborka, at one time served as a jail. The first prisoner, after whom it was then named, was the knight Dalibor of Kozojedy.

There was no way to pass the long hours in the harsh prison and Dalibor feared he would fall to dark thoughts, but he loved music and so he decided to ask the jailer to procure a violin for him.

As soon as he drew the first notes from it his mood lifted; after a time he tried out his own melodies and he played and played. Time passed, and Dalibor became a virtuoso on the violin and there was no one who could compare to him. Even the jailers, who were no connoisseurs, liked to listen to his mournful tunes, as did the people who would gather by the tower under the prisoner's window.

At that time the food in the prison was very poor, in fact there was almost none, and Dalibor constantly suffered from hunger. One of the jailers took pity on him and gave him a good piece of advice:

"Don't be a fool, every day there are people listening beneath your window. They have come to love your music, so ask them for a bit of grub. They won't miss it and it will do you good."

The idea was a good one. The next day a bag attached to a rope slid out of the window before the eyes of the gathered listeners. The people guessed what it was meant for and began to regularly drop in a bit of food here, something to drink there, and even the odd coin. In this way, Dalibor began to make a decent livelihood for himself with his playing.

But all good things come to an end. The judges, who were led in their deliberations by fears about their property and worries about further riots among their subjects, passed an exemplary judgment on Dalibor: beheading by the sword. The judgment was executed promptly, under the Old Castle Steps.

The fate of the knight Dalibor of Kozojedy was imprinted on the minds of the people, who passed it on from generation to generation, until it was eventually popularised in the well-known Czech proverb: "necessity taught Dalibor to play", meaning approximately the same as the English "necessity is the mother of invention".

PALEČEK THE JESTER

King George of Poděbrady also had a favourite jester. Because of his small stature he was called Paleček (Little Thumb). He was clever and just and always stood up for the poor, who had no way to appeal to the authorities.

The wealthy, however, claimed that he was vain, because he very often turned up in new clothing. But there was a reason for this: whenever Paleček met a poor, ill-dressed person, he gave them his clothes. He travelled around country farmsteads and when it was needed, he would help fix a roof or fence, never wanting anything in return or even taking a meal for his troubles. He managed to defend the rights of the innocent before the king, always with humour and insight. When he received some money, he immediately gave it away to the needy.

Once, a great banquet was being held at the royal court to honour some distinguished guests. Delicious specialities were served, in particular, select types of fish. But these were only served at the table for the noble guests; those of lesser houses had to be content with tiny loaches. Paleček sat in his customary spot by the door, where only the small fish were served. With a completely straight face he chose the tiniest fish of them all and put it up to his ear. "Little sister fish, have you heard anything about my brother?" he whispered

and listened for a moment. He gave a disappointed sigh, returned the fish to the bowl and picked out another. He posed the same question, "Little sister fish, have you heard anything about my brother?" Again he listened for a moment, sadly murmured his disappointment, and again returned it to the bowl, repeating this strange interrogation several more times. The guests around him were enjoying themselves immensely, laughing and joking, until the strange commotion around Paleček caught the attention of the king himself. And because he knew his jester very well, he knew that this was not just a bit of comedy. He summoned Paleček and asked him for an explanation.

"Well, you see, my King, I had a brother who was a fisherman, and years ago he drowned in the river. I asked people if they knew anything about him but they told me nothing. So now I'm asking the fish if maybe they...," Paleček responded with a grave face.

"And what have you learned?" the king asked, amused.

Paleček gave an even sadder look and slyly complained: "Nothing, my King. The little fish say they are too small to remember something like that. They say I should ask the bigger ones from your table."

The king immediately guessed where Paleček's act was going and he ordered the biggest fish to be taken to the tables by the door too. Indeed, he was accustomed to the fact that his wise jester always did well to remind him that a ruler's main duty is to be just to all his subjects.

It is said, and it is not unbelievable, that after Paleček's death, the king also soon parted from this earthly life and went to join his faithful servant, his good and just court jester.

The Cathedral of St Vitus, St Wenceslas and St Adalbert

THE ST VITUS BELLS

It is said that the St Vitus bells can change their sounds according to the mood of the nation. It is also said that the bells cannot be stolen from the tower because any thief would instantly die and, moreover, the bells loaded on a cart would weigh it down so much that it wouldn't move. And even if someone did manage it, the bells would eventually fly back to the cathedral's south tower themselves.

It is as if the St Vitus bells had a soul and were connected to the Czech nation at personal moments as well. When the Emperor and Bohemian King Charles IV was dying, the death knell began to ring in the tower of St Vitus Cathedral all by itself. The King heard it and called: "Lo, my children, the Lord our God is calling me, let me be with him forever!"

The son of Charles IV, Wenceslas, feared the south tower, where the bells are located. An astrologer had predicted that he would die "before the St Vitus tower". That prophecy haunted him day and night.

"I order that the south tower of the cathedral be torn down," King Wenceslas decided in an effort to outwit his fate. Before the masons managed to destroy the tower completely, however, death struck the king unexpectedly. Only on his deathbed did Wenceslas grasp the true meaning of the prophecy, "that his demise would come before the tower is destroyed".

THE ZIKMUND BELL AND THE ROPE OF HUMAN HAIR

The first and largest of the St Vitus bells is named Zikmund. It measures over two metres and weighs more than sixteen tonnes. When the bell-makers cast it in 1549, no one knew how to lift it up into the St Vitus tower. Neither ropes nor cords could bear it, they snapped like tiny threads.

The king watched these attempts with concern from his chamber.

"Father," said his daughter, coming to him, "do not worry, I will come up with something and you will see that we will get the bell into the tower."

"I am surprised, daughter, but I know you and I know that your cleverness surpasses many a royal sage. I trust you," the king agreed.

The king's daughter shut herself in her chambers for a time and began to draw up plans day and night for assembling a machine that would pull Zikmund up to the tower. She also called together all her friends and together they began to braid a strong rope out of human hair. Workers then assembled a machine according to her draft.

On the day that the device was to be used, people gathered around it to see the miracle, but they had strong doubts about it:

"A rope made of human hair cannot hold the weight of such a heavy bell. It will break and Zikmund will smash into a thousand pieces."

Then there was nothing left for them to do but watch in amazement as the taut, glossy rope lifted the valuable weight without the slightest problem up into the belfry. Beneath the tower a thunderous applause erupted and everyone had words of admiration and respect for the king's daughter.

It is said that the clapper of this gigantic bell is fragile, and if it were to break, the Czech lands would be in danger. This legend turned out to be true very recently.

Zikmund's clapper cracked in 2002 and two months later the Czech Republic was hit by the flood of the millennium.

THE MIRACULOUS HELM OF PRINCE WENCESLAS

The greatest holiday for Prague residents used to be the transporting of the remains of Prince Wenceslas. And so it happened that two foreign archers who lived in the Golden Lane were standing in the courtyard in front of St Vitus Cathedral on the day before this holiday. One of them cursed in frustration:

"Why should I celebrate this holiday? I didn't celebrate it at home and I won't here either. I'm just losing out on wages."

At that moment he froze, then staggered, waving his hands around and calling out desperately:

"Is there anyone there? Why is it suddenly so dark? Where are you? Help! Light – I need a light!" he repeated miserably and groped the air around him.

"Quit joking around! Have you gone mad? It's daytime," the second archer said, trying to calm him. But he was terrified because he had heard many times that Saint Wenceslas cruelly punishes those who sin against his memory.

"My God, I've gone blind!"

People began to gather and, taking pity, led him to the master of medicine. But medicine did not help, nor did herbs or ointments. Everything was in vain.

"Only Saint Wenceslas can help you. Have yourself led to his grave, repent your insult and beg for forgiveness," someone advised.

The people led the soldier to the grave, where he knelt in prayer and begged for forgiveness. Nothing happened, however: he remained veiled in pitch black darkness.

"Place the helm of Saint Wenceslas on his head!" called out the voice of an old priest who had just entered the Chapel of St Wenceslas. They did so. They removed the precious helm from its case and placed it on the blinded foreigner's head.

As if awaking from a dream he regained his sight. He bowed to St Wenceslas and thanked him. From that time he never again missed the celebrations of St Wenceslas.

Strahov Monastery

THE PIOUS ABBOT

The Strahov Abbot Lohel had to travel a lot in order to oversee the Premonstratensian monasteries, even those outside Bohemia as well. Once, when he was returning to Prague and wanted to pay to stay the night at an inn near Krumlov, he discovered he had nothing to pay with, because in his goodness he had given all his money to the poor. And so he agreed with the innkeeper:

"I shall leave my abbot's cross with its gold chain here as collateral. You will return it to the one who brings the money and identifies himself with my abbot's ring."

In Prague, an urgent message from the emperor himself was waiting for the abbot, summoning him to come immediately over an urgent matter. The abbot was filled with dread: how could he go before the emperor without his abbot's cross? Should he lie that he was sick? He couldn't. And so he began to pray to Saint Elizabeth, the protector of those in distress. In the morning he caught sight of his abbot's cross with its gold chain on the faldstool. Amazed, he inquired who had brought it, but no one knew. The only witness was the innkeeper, who said the deposit had been paid off by a wealthy lady who had presented the abbot's signet ring.

"As she was riding away I watched her go. At the crossroads her horses and carriage rose up to the heavens and disappeared from sight," the innkeeper recounted.

"It was none other than Saint Elizabeth," the abbot exclaimed.

After that, he had a hospital for the poor built in her honour at Pohořelec.

THE SKELETON'S JUSTICE

When the Swedish captured Prague, Hradčany and Malá Strana, not only did they rob and pillage the townhouses, but they also fell upon the churches and monasteries. They looted Strahov Monastery so thoroughly that there was nothing left but the tin and lead coffins from the graves under the church. They robbed the dead and melted down the coffins in order to have enough money for gambling. And they needed plenty of it!

One Swedish mercenary lost everything he had and so he once again began searching the place where he was staying – Strahov Monastery.

There was nothing left that he could turn into cash. The tombs had been picked clean, there was no sign left of the golden church receptacles, the sacred vestments had been sliced up… Then the Swede noticed a tomb in an unusual place – in the lower passage in front of the sacristy. The stone was intact, which the Swede took to mean that it hadn't been robbed yet.

He waited until all the mercenaries in the monastery had fallen asleep so he wouldn't have to share his loot with anyone else, and around midnight he set out for the tomb. The tombstone was fairly easy to remove; he inserted a wooden beam and entered the tomb holding a lantern. He removed the lid from the tin coffin and shone the light inside to see if the body was wearing any gold rings or valuable jewellery, but he didn't even manage to get a look.

Bang! Thud! A deafening boom rang out behind him. The beam snapped and the mighty tombstone closed again. The mercenary did not even have time to be startled – a skeletal hand was already closing around his throat and choking him. He wanted to defend himself and call for help, but not a sound came out, so deadly strong was the skeleton's grasp.

The inhabitants of the Monastery noticed the cracked tombstone the next day, but did not pay much attention to it – the Swedish pillaging had resulted in untold damage. But the Swedes were looking for their comrade.

Only when the Swedish soldiers had left and everything had returned more or less to normal at the monastery did the abbot order the cracked tombstone to be replaced. And what did they find in the tomb! The Swedish mercenary on his knees by the coffin and a skeleton leaning out of the coffin grasping his neck. So strong was the skeleton's grasp that they could barely extract the Swede.

Loreta Square

SIGNATURE FROM BEYOND THE GRAVE

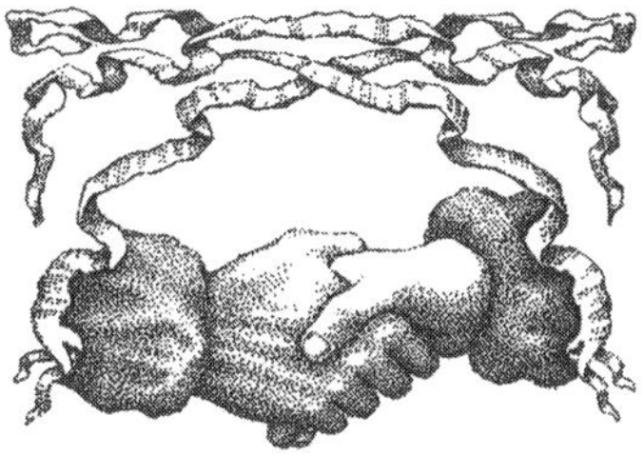

The rich Count Czernin decided that he would have a spectacular palace built on Loreta Square. For a long time he sought out a builder who would take on such a bold project. In the end he found one. The count paid him a decent sum as a deposit and the builder could start working. He spared no expense, the work was truly worth it. Soon the deposit had been spent and the builder had to use his own savings, but he had no doubt that the generous count would honour his debt.

The palace was nearly finished when the builder learned of a devastating bit of news – Count Czernin had unexpectedly died. Out of respect for the deceased, the builder waited until the countess's period of mourning had ended, and then he set out to present all the unpaid bills to her.

"Show me the signed consent of my husband to such great expenses," the countess demanded.

"I have nothing in hand; the count and I agreed with a handshake," the builder protested.

"Then I consider the expenses for the building settled with the deposit paid," the countess declared adamantly.

Seeing that nothing would convince the countess, the builder began to think about what he should do and to whom he should turn.

It occurred to him that his brother was a member of the secret society of Freemasons. He will certainly come up with something, the builder thought hopefully.

And so he did.

The brother led the builder to the Freemason members and they promised to help him.

"Write up the contract just as you agreed with the count," the grand master advised. He then uttered arcane words over the covenants for some time, then gestured toward the curtain that conccaled the great hall. From behind the curtain emerged Count Czernin, who waved to the builder as if sleepwalking and placed his right hand on the document in the place designated for his signature. He held the hand there a moment, then disappeared as suddenly as he had appeared.

The builder stared in amazement at Czernin's handprint on the contract but, wasting no more time, he thanked them politely, said goodbye to the Freemasons and his brother and set out to see the countess.

The countess looked long and hard at the document with the imprint of her husband's hand, but she then had the remaining amount paid out to the builder down to the last penny.

BREAD CRUST SLIPPERS

A rich and beautiful countess lived at Czernin Palace on Loreta Square. She was also proud and vain. Her extravagance knew no bounds. Every day she needed to show off in the most beautiful dress, every evening in a different one, and she flaunted jewellery, rare fabrics and the most wondrous gemstones. She liked to dazzle men and invoke envy in women. She did nothing other than spend the whole day thinking about what new things to wear and what original pieces with which to fascinate so that no other woman would have anything that could compare.

And so it happened that an unusual extravagance occurred to her. She had a baker and a shoemaker called in.

"For tomorrow's ball you are to make me slippers made of bread crust," she instructed them. "They should be soft and supple, so they are easy to dance in."

Both were shocked at the countess's fancy. "My lady! It is not right to tread on bread crust, to say nothing of dancing on it. Bread is the gift of God."

"It is my order. If you do not want this task, another baker and shoemaker will be happy to do it for me!"

The baker and shoemaker did not resist the countess's order any more – they had too many children and debts – and they set to work. It went well. The next day they were already holding a fine pair of slippers.

At the ball the curious ladies wondered in vain from what exotic material the countess's new slippers had been made. The countess herself was satisfied to the extreme. Dressed in muslin and silk, in her slippers of bread crust, she received the envious looks with satisfaction and rose off the ground with pride in the dance.

"Excuse me, countess, may I hope that you will honour me with the next dance?" asked a handsome cavalier in black, a tall foreigner with sparkling, glowing eyes, bowing elegantly before the countess.

The countess, drunk on the overwhelming admiration of all the guests and the eloquent words of the handsome stranger, gave her consent and in the thrill of the dance did not even notice that the dance steps of the mysterious stranger were leading her out of the ballroom, inconspicuously approaching the entrance to the palace dungeons. The countess halted. As if suddenly sobering up from the deceptive intoxication, she looked upon the dancer's face. He was no longer smiling, but holding her tightly, even roughly, by the hand, pulling her down the stairs to the dungeons. On the last step he let her go.

"You debauched woman! You thought you could escape punishment? Look at your slippers!" the stranger cried, now revealed as the Devil. The countess reeled. She looked down at her bread crust slippers and saw they were laced with tiny flames that were growing in strength, shooting up around her and turning her legs into a living hell. The countess shrieked in pain and horror, trying to take off the slippers, but she was already surrounded from all sides by the infernal flames, licking at her until they consumed her entirely.

Sometimes quick uncertain steps sound out from the dungeons of Czernin Palace as the proud countess tries to escape from her sinful act, fleeing the flames of hell that always catch up with her in retribution.

THE SINGING LORETA BELLS

It is said that the bells in the tower at the Loreta began to sing during one tragic event.

A poor widow lived on a small street in Nový Svět at that time. She had as many children as there were bells at the Loreta and thus she used to call them “my little Loreta bells”.

She had the same number of silver coins stored away for them, which she had once received from a wealthy relative. She wanted to give them one coin each once they came of age.

Man proposes, God disposes. Prague was struck by a contagious plague which chose its victims primarily among the poor. The poor widow’s family did not go unaffected. The first to fall ill was the oldest son. The desperate mother did not even have enough to pay a doctor, but she wanted to at least pay for a funeral. She took down the string on which the money was strung, removed the first coin and took it to Loreta. Not long after that the bell announcing the death of the young boy sounded from Loreta. The widow had hardly finished burying the first child when another fell sick, then another and another... Each time the widow took a coin down from the string and each time a bell at Loreta rang – each time a smaller bell until the smallest rang when the youngest child was buried.

With pain in her heart she returned to her empty home, the heat rising in her cheeks. She felt that she too had fallen ill.

“My beloved children,” she wept, “I saw you all off, but who will toll for me on my final journey?”

Hardly had she finished saying it when all the bells rang out from the Loreta tower. They played and sang so beautifully that people wept, moved by the magnificent melody.

The widow smiled with joy, for she understood that she would not be alone on her final journey.

Charles Bridge

PARLER'S RECIPE

Prague's oldest bridge has changed its appearance many times over the ages as a result of frequent flooding. The banks of the Vltava were originally connected by a wooden bridge. When floods carried it away, it was replaced by a stone bridge in 1172, named Judith's Bridge after the wife of King Vladislav II. But it, too, failed to withstand flooding in 1342 and fell apart.

Charles IV entrusted the construction of a new stone bridge to the renowned Peter Parler. So that the bridge would be strong and resistant, he had the builders mix lime with wine and raw eggs into the mortar. After a time it became clear that there would not be enough eggs in all of Prague for the structure, and thus the king ordered all Bohemian towns to help out with the construction.

Before long, wooden carts lined with straw and loaded with baskets and crates full of eggs were heading to Prague. Often the masons did not even have to crack them, as the bumpy trip had done their work for them and yolks and whites were already dripping from the carts before they got into the city.

"But the eggs will break on us on the way, we'd better hard-boil them before the trip," the inhabitants of Velvary concluded reasonably, ensuring long years of mirth in Prague with their act.

But they weren't alone. The conscientious residents of Unhošť apparently misunderstood the royal edict and, in addition to milk, also sent fresh cheese and curds. These special ingredients both intentionally and inadvertently made the Charles Bridge immortal.

PERUN'S SWORD

Under Charles Bridge on the bank of the Vltava there used to be a sacred grove with a great statue to the god Perun, who was brandishing a sword. With the end of paganism the people cleared the grove and at the place where they toppled the statue of Perun into the river, a deep pool formed. When building Charles Bridge the stonemasons walled Perun's sword in among the stones. Where exactly, they never said, and no one knows today.

Perun never forgave the people for toppling his likeness and he would lie in wait at the bottom of the Vltava for lone fishermen or swimmers so he could pull them down into the pool where the Praguers had thrown him.

"It is best to avoid the pool and go around it," cautioned those who lived on the banks of the Vltava. "Even if some unfortunate soul calls for help, it is wise to wait until they emerge somewhere further along."

Every time Perun claimed a victim, he would be satisfied for a time and the waters around the pool would calm.

Time carried away the tale of Perun and his appetite for victims, but Perun's sword hidden among the stones of Charles Bridge still troubles the curious today.

PRINCE BRUNCVÍK AND THE MAGIC SWORD

The Czech lands were once ruled by the honest and righteous Prince Bruncvík. One day he decided to change his coat of arms – a black eagle on a golden field, which he had inherited from his father. He wanted to have the lion, as the king of all animals, in his emblem.

He prepared to travel and promised his wife that he would return within seven years, exchanging rings with her as a sign of his promise.

Prince Bruncvík and his entourage travelled through unknown lands, crossed wild seas and, during one unusually violent storm, his ship was wrecked on a deserted island. All of Bruncvík's crew died of hunger and thirst there, leaving behind only the prince and a single devout knight.

"My Prince, the only hope for you is the Roc, which comes once in a while looking for prey on this island. I will sew you and your sword into a horse's hide smeared in blood and plant you on a high rock so the Roc cannot miss you."

He did as he had said and everything went according to plan. The bird came, saw the bloody hide, seized it and only dropped it once it reached land to feed its young.

Bruncvík freed himself from his foul-smelling prison with his sword and set out through the unknown land, not knowing where he was going. For nine days he wandered through the wild mountains and forests until he reached a deep valley from which horrible cries of pain were emanating. The king of the animals was on its last legs fighting against a nine-headed hydra. Bruncvík wasted no time and sprang to the lion's aid. Almost completely exhausted, they finally managed to kill the beast together. The lion became Bruncvík's faithful companion and never abandoned him, standing ever by his side, even in the fiercest of battles.

Indeed, he needed it. They experienced many an adventure together, freeing a princess from the clutches of a dragon and through trickery obtaining a magic sword that needed only to be pulled from its scabbard and the heads of all enemies would fall off. Such a sword came in very handy. Bruncvík used it many times on his travels to save his life, many times uttering the sentence: "All heads off!"

Finally, after a long journey, he returned to Prague. All were overjoyed. They admired his brave and faithful lion and eagerly painted him on the city's walls and gates – a lion on a red field. And so Bruncvík's wish to have a lion, the king of all animals, on the coat of arms of the Kingdom of Bohemia was fulfilled.

Bruncvík ruled with his wife for many more years, and when he died, his faithful lion died as well.

In order to honour the memory of the good prince, Prague's inhabitants erected a statue of Bruncvík with a stone lion on a pillar of Charles Bridge. He remains there today, though what happened to his magic sword is unknown. One legend states that Bruncvík had his sword encased in one of the pillars of the bridge. It will allegedly appear when the Czech lands are at their worst. The Knights of Blaník will awake in the mountain of the same name with Saint Wenceslas leading them, and when they are riding across Charles Bridge his horse will stumble on the stone under which the sword is hidden. St Wenceslas will take the sword, swing it above his head and the Czech lands will be free of all enemies.

THE DEVIL'S RUSE

Associating with the Devil never brought anyone any happiness, that's a well-known thing. One such instance took place when the statue of John of Nepomuk was taken down from Charles Bridge. On the same night the bridge's arch collapsed and no one could repair it, because whatever the masons repaired during the day would disappear into the Vltava in the night. Everyone was at a loss – whatever they did, they could not repair the bridge. Then a young builder turned up, full of ambition and determined to get the bridge back in order.

"I shall hire the best masons and by nightfall half the work will be done," the builder assured. When darkness fell, he hid on the bridge and watched to see what would happen. At midnight there was a crash and the half-finished work collapsed into the Vltava. The Devil himself stood in the middle of the bridge and cackled at the destruction.

"Your work is in vain," the Devil laughed at the builder. "Of course, there is one way out," he added with a sly grin.

"What do you want?" the builder asked straight away, eager for fame and recognition and already thinking about how to outwit the Devil.

"I will take the first to cross the repaired bridge."

The Devil kept his promise: the bridge stayed repaired. Work on the bridge ended, the bridge was to be consecrated and the builder ordered that no one was to be allowed on to the bridge until he himself permitted it. At dawn he was planning to drive a rooster across the bridge before him and thus outwit the Devil.

But the Devil saw through his trap. He disguised himself as a mason and set out to visit the builder's wife.

"Your husband is in great danger! He asks that you come to him straight away," the Devil lied.

The guards did not think to stop the builder's wife, and greeted her respectfully instead. The wife ran across the bridge, overcome with anxiety at what had happened to her husband and calling out his name from a distance.

The builder froze. What a grave mistake he had made, thinking he could outwit the Devil. But he pretended nothing was the matter and walked his wife back home. He came back to the repaired arch and waited for the Devil, prepared to sacrifice himself instead. But the Devil had not shown up by morning. So the builder headed home, but terrible news was waiting for him there: in the night his wife had given birth to a dead baby and she herself had also died.

The builder's conscience suffered, having caused the death of both wife and child, and soon his soul, too, went over to the other world. But from that time there was no peace on Charles Bridge. Those who crossed the bridge at night could hear the sneezing of a frozen newborn hovering over the bridge. Usually they would just quicken their pace without looking around.

Once a man from the country was passing through and heard the sneezing behind him.

"God bless you!" he called out politely and hurried on.

"And you too," sounded a child's voice in response.

And from then on there has been peace on Charles Bridge.

TWO DREAMS AND ONE TREASURE

Once a poor man, who had a wife, many children, a small cottage, a small garden, in it a young apple tree, and more worries about supporting them all than one man could bear, had a strange dream: that he was crossing a stone bridge in Prague, tripped over a cobblestone and underneath it found some golden treasure. The next night the cottager had the same dream. And when he had the exact same dream on the third night as well, he could hold out no longer and in the morning set out to Prague, heading right for Charles Bridge. He walked back and forth, looking around, wanting most of all to turn over every single stone, but he found nothing.

"I couldn't have had that dream for no reason at all, it must've been a sign, it must come true somehow," the cottager muttered to himself with his head down as he explored every crevice on the bridge.

"I say, good man, I've been watching you for a while now. What were you searching for all that time, yesterday?" a soldier from the guard booth in the middle of the bridge asked the cottager.

"I'm searching for some golden treasure I dreamt about three nights in a row," sighed the disappointed cottager, and told the soldier everything.

"How strange," the soldier wondered, "I too had a similar dream about golden treasure three nights in a row, but mine was buried under a young apple tree in a small garden by a small cottage."

The cottager couldn't believe his ears when the soldier described the place from his dream in detail.

"Why, that's my cottage, my garden and my young apple tree," he said, astonished. As soon as the soldier's shift ended, they set out together for the village where the cottager lived: to the cottage, and into the garden where they began to dig under the young apple tree. It did not take long – under a thin layer of sod they hit upon a chest full of gold and silver. They divided up the treasure fairly, and so both of their dreams about the golden treasure came true.

PUNISHED PRIDE

Beggars used to sit by the cross on Charles Bridge asking passers-by for alms. A very wealthy woman who owned a large estate, several palaces in Prague, many merchant ships on the Elbe and Vltava, and a chateau in the country, used to pass by, but she never even looked down at the beggars.

Once, a ragged old beggar woman stretched out her hands to the lady and said:

"Have mercy, madam, on my poverty. I too was once like you."

The proud woman passed by her with contempt.

The beggar woman called after her:

"Have mercy and God will have mercy on you as well."

"I have no need of God's mercy. I have so much of everything that I could buy the whole kingdom if I wanted," the lady retorted angrily.

A guard, who was standing nearby, heard the rich woman's scornful words and could not keep silent:

"Do not insult God, madam, you never know when he will punish you with poverty."

"What are you pattering about, you wretch?" the woman said, angry at the soldier now as well. "Look at this precious ring I am taking off and throwing into the Vltava before your eyes. It will come back to me sooner than your words about my poverty come to pass!" The lady laughed and threw the ring in the river.

Several days later she organised a great banquet at her seat, and as part of the feast the chef ordered local fish. When he was cleaning and gutting them, he pulled a shiny object out of one of them and discovered to his surprise that it was the ring of his lady. He immediately ran to her and when he showed her the ring she turned white as a sheet.

The profecy came to pass.

A few days later all her boats sank, her countryside estates burnt down and her chateau was plundered by robbers. And so the wealthy lady suddenly became a desperate beggar.

She was discovered her on the bridge among the other beggars under the cross, but she was already dead.

KING WENCESLAS AND BRAVE ZUZANA

King Wenceslas had been imprisoned by the nobles for four months already, and he was beginning to lose hope that he would manage to get free and escape from his prison. He was very closely watched.

Summer came. The sun baked the stones of Prague and the heat was overwhelming. King Wenceslas asked his jailers if he could refresh himself in the city baths by Charles Bridge. They agreed, but strong guards accompanied him.

Following his bath, the king exited onto a small adjoining balcony where the baths' laundry was drying. He looked sadly at the Castle and, with bleak thoughts, looked off down the current of the Vltava. His eyes fell on a rowboat that was tied up just below the balcony.

At that moment a young barber girl came out to put away the dry laundry. The king motioned to her and she approached him.

"My name is Zuzana, my King, and I am devoted to you with all my heart. How can I serve you?" Zuzana bowed with these words and awaited the king's wish.

"Do you see that boat?" the king pointed. "If you know how to row, take me to the other bank of the river and I will reward you generously."

Zuzana did not hesitate for a moment. She tied together several sheets, they climbed down them to the boat and Zuzana quickly and deftly rowed into the trees and bushes on the opposite bank. There they remained hidden until the furore over the king's disappearance from the baths had calmed, and set out along the bank against the current of the river.

King Wenceslas was saved and free. In time, his conflicts with the provincial lords were settled and he could return to the Castle to rule for several more years to the satisfaction of all.

He did not forget about brave Zuzana. Apart from paying her one hundred gold coins right away, he had a new baths built in place of the old ones by Charles Bridge and gave them to Zuzana along with a generous annuity. He raised barbering to the level of an honoured trade and allowed barbers to use a new sign: a kingfisher on a golden field surrounded by a coiled towel. He then had the image of brave Zuzana painted on the vault of the bridge tower in her honour. She is easy to recognise: she is holding a tub in her left hand and in her right a coiled towel.

The Church of Our Lady of Victory

THE INFANT JESUS OF PRAGUE

In 1628, the Czech noblewoman, Polyxena of Lobkowicz, known for her mercy, gave the Carmelites in Malá Strana a small wax statue of the Infant Jesus. The Carmelites prayed to the statue when things were at their worst, when they were hungry and did not even have a hunk of bread.

The statue soon became very popular, especially among the sick, even overshadowing the altarpiece of Our Lady of Victory.

When foreign armies tore into Prague in 1631, they did not spare the Carmelite church and monastery. One of the soldiers also touched the statue, but with such little care that he broke off its hand, which he then threw in a pile of trash along with the rest of the statue.

One of the Carmelite brothers found the lost statue after seven long years. He returned it to its pedestal in the church with joy and in his excitement did not even notice that the hand had been broken off.

"Have mercy on me and I will have mercy on you!" a voice suddenly said.

Only then did he notice that the statue was missing a piece of hand under the sleeve. He immediately began seeking out an artist who could fix the statue, but the job turned out to be more difficult than he had expected. No matter who redid the hand, it would always fall off by the next day. The reason was that those who repaired the statue had committed many sins in their lives. Until one day, when a young artist came to the monastery asking if he could repair the statue.

The prior agreed and the young artist set to work. He worked kneeling as if in prayer to the statue. As soon as he had finished the job, he disappeared from the monastery like a ghost, without waiting for his payment.

The news spread throughout all of Prague that the statue was back in its place in the church, and legions of devotees flocked to it.

Year by year devotion to the Infant Jesus grew and even spread beyond the borders of the Czech lands. The place of prayer was never empty. Even the Carmelites never left its side, even at night.

But then a cruel winter came, half of Prague fell ill and the Carmelite monastery was turned into a hospital. With his last strength the prior ran the monastery and, very weary, just before midnight, he set out to kneel before the Infant Jesus.

He entered the church and was amazed: the altar around the Infant Jesus was crowded with candles and kneeling beneath it were seven angels.

Next day the prior asked the sexton to replace the candles around the Infant Jesus – they must have burnt down during the night. It turned out, however, that they had not diminished at all, to say nothing of having burnt down – it was as if someone had placed new ones there.

These and other miracles took place around the Infant Jesus of Prague, and they still do today. His admirers have not waned in number.

The Old Town Astronomical Clock

MASTER HANUŠ

The Old Town Astronomical Clock was built by medieval clockmaker Mikuláš of Kadaň roughly before 1410. Jan of Růže, also known as Master Hanuš, added the separate calendar disc to it at the end of the 15th century and improved the wheel train, making it a truly unique work admired by all the people as well as renowned master clockmakers.

Prague's councillors were also satisfied, but also wary, because the fame of the Old Town Astronomical Clock crossed the country's borders and learned men and experts from abroad started arriving to visit Master Hanuš. And because the master almost never left his room and was constantly sketching, calculating and making notes, the councillors judged that he was designing a new astronomical clock, even more perfect, for a city in France. And because they wanted only Prague to have such a unique machine, they began to discuss how to stop Master Hanuš.

"We will make him sign a pledge that he will never make such an astronomical clock again," one of the councillors proposed.

"Or we will make him swear it right in front of everyone," another proposed. But none of the ideas seemed safe enough.

"If we want to have the most beautiful and best astronomical clock in the world, there is only one way to prevent Master Hanuš from continuing his work," proposed one particularly tough and jealous councillor. "We will take his sight. He shall live, but he will no longer draw new designs – he simply won't be able to see them, gentlemen. And we will ensure that he has everything he needs for the rest of his life. That is a sensible solution."

The councillors resisted, they were afraid, but the alderman defended his solution until he had convinced everyone.

It was late at night. Master Hanuš was still sitting at his table and working. His maid and assistant had long since departed, when suddenly there was a loud knocking at the door.

Such strange knocking at this late time of night, the master thought, rising from his work to bar the door, but he was too late. Two masked men burst through the door, grabbed Hanuš and threw him on the ground, whereupon he lost consciousness.

No one knows what happened next, but when his assistant arrived the next morning, he found his master feverish, delirious and blindfolded.

"A light, I need a light," Hanuš was calling confusedly.

The assistant called in the neighbours and together they took the gauze off the master's eyes. They froze in horror: instead of eyes Hanuš had only empty sockets, still bloody from the hot iron.

Master Hanuš was sick for a long time, only lying in bed struggling with the question of who had done this to him and for what reason. He began to wonder whether it had really been human hands that had blinded him, thinking it must have been dark forces that were punishing him for his work. The master's assistant divulged that it was being said that the culprits of this evil act were not too far off, though no one would ever find them.

Master Hanuš finally understood "why", and after a time he asked his assistant to lead him to the astronomical clock, to the most complex part of the wheel train. At the very moment when the statue of Death pulled on the bell rope, Master Hanuš grabbed hold of the wooden lever and pulled with all his might. The machine gave a grinding screech and Death stopped ringing the bell. Master Hanuš fell to the ground and breathed his last.

The astronomical clock's machine stopped and remained silent for years, because no one could be found who could repair it.

THE SKELETON'S POWER

The statue of the Skeleton (also called Death) has strange powers. When the astronomical clock's train is broken and it stops showing the time, bad times fall upon the Czech nation and the Skeleton marks this with the first nod of his head. The only one who can break this power is a boy who was born in the night on New Year's Eve.

The boy must run from Týn Church toward the astronomical clock at the moment the Skeleton first nods his head, make it across the Old Town Square, and reach the Old Town Hall before the last hour strikes. Only if the boy manages this will the Skeleton's power be broken forever.

THE PRISONER AND THE SPARROW

The two little windows above the clock once led to a jail cell for noble-born prisoners.

Once, a knight, who had been sentenced to death, found himself in the cell. He was waiting for the executioner to come and carry out his work. He sulked, looking out dejectedly at the square through the little window.

The clock began to strike the hour and Death shook his scythe and opened his jaws. Just when his jaws were opened at their widest, a sparrow flew in. The jaws snapped shut and trapped the sparrow for the whole of the next hour. When the astronomical clock began to chime again, Death opened his jaws and the sparrow flew out like a shot and disappeared over the roofs of the buildings opposite.

The prisoner watched all this from his window. He compared the sparrow's fate to his own and when the sparrow left his prison, a glimmer of hope shone in the knight that he too might be saved.

And so it was – on the same day the city granted him a pardon.

Old Town Square

THE TWENTY-SEVEN EXECUTED

In 1621, twenty-seven Czech lords were executed on the Old Town Square for participating in the estates rebellion against the rule of Ferdinand II. The twenty-seven crosses made of white cobblestones by the Old Town Astronomical Clock commemorate this sad event. No one knows where their bodies were interred, though their heads were hung in iron baskets on the Bridge Tower by Charles Bridge as a warning, and it was a long time before their relatives were allowed to take them away.

Every year on the anniversary of their execution on 21 June, the shadows of all twenty-seven executed Czech lords meet at the site of that horrible event, by the Old Town Hall. They stand and mournfully watch the astronomical clock.

If it is running correctly and accurately, the twenty-seven shadows judge that the Czech nation is doing well, and they depart in peace.

If the machine is broken or the time is wrong, they can tell right away that something is wrong with the Czech nation as well. In this case, they leave in deep sorrow and wait for another year to pass.

THE IMMURED CHILD

Construction of the Kinský Palace on the Old Town Square dragged on for a long time. It was held up by disputes with the city over the chosen site, but above all by the slow pace of work.

No wonder, when every new wall they built in the palace collapsed. The builders, masters and masons were all desperate. Then someone remembered the old tradition used by castle builders, they would immure an innocent girl or boy in the foundations. Such a castle was then impregnable.

This cruel custom was later abandoned and a rooster was walled into castle or town walls instead.

There was no rooster wandering around the Old Town Square, but there were many ragged children no one would miss. And so the masons immured a stray child into the walls of the palace.

From that moment no newly built wall collapsed, the work ran smoothly and the construction of the palace was soon complete.

To this day, this extremely beautiful Rococo palace stands out proudly among the other buildings on the square and no one has a clue that an innocent child is buried among its foundations.

Ungelt

THE SMITTEN TURK

The paths of traders from around the world, including those of Turks, used to lead to Ungelt.

One of those who travelled to Prague's Ungelt was exceptionally handsome. Young, tall, with dark fiery eyes, and moreover extremely rich. This Turk happened to fall in love with the young daughter of the innkeeper there. She had a gentle face, forget-me-not eyes and long blonde hair tied in a braid.

Long did she shy from the Turk's bewitching gaze, but the gentle manner with which he always approached her convinced her in the end. Their affection was mutual, and it seemed that nothing would stand in the way of their marriage. The girl's father, however, wished for the wedding to take place in Prague. The Turk agreed, but had to return to his own country for his own consent to wed.

"I give you this precious piece of jewellery, my most beautiful, with the faith that you will wait patiently," said the Turk, tying an exquisite necklace around the girl's neck. He said good-bye and hurried off to his homeland.

Time passed, and the Turk did not return. The girl first told herself that his journey was long, then that he had forgotten about her, and then her memory of him was lost in the mists of time.

As she was a beautiful girl, she had no lack of suitors, and because she did not wish to remain an old maid, in the end she married the son of a merchant from the neighbourhood.

One day, in the heat of summer, the Turkish groom appeared unexpectedly at Ungelt. He had come back for his bride. He ran to the girl's home full of joy and great desire – what agony he felt when he learned that his bride had not waited for him and had married another. He gave no sign of his woe, however, and merely asked her:

"Young madam, how extremely glad I would be if you could take a moment so I could talk with you," and pretended he would be leaving Prague soon.

She hesitated, but in the end she decided to fulfil his wish and went to visit the Turk at the inn where he was staying. The poor soul did not know what she was in for. The Turk could not get over the fact that his betrothed preferred another, and so he punished her according to his own rules: he chopped off the girl's head, buried the body in the cellar and placed her head in a precious cabinet.

Because he could not bear to be separated from her, he took the head with him in the little chest wherever he went as his greatest treasure.

The girl's ghost followed him everywhere however, and from the box he could hear her wails wherever he travelled.

He could bear it no longer. He decided to return to Prague and deposit the girl's head where he had buried her body.

When he had done so, he left Prague in disguise.

Much water flowed down the Vltava, and people forgot about the young innkeeper's daughter and the rich Turk, but from time to time someone would colour their tale with this sad story.

Once, in the deep of night, a young tailor was returning home via Ungelt. He was just passing the entrance to the old cellar when a man stepped out of the shadows in a silk coat with a turban on his head. He nodded to him and passed by. The tailor saw in the man's hand a woman's head with a long blonde braid. He wanted to scream, but he was unable. He just turned and fled from Ungelt toward the Old Town Square.

From that time the Turk has appeared to random night walkers. Usually he emerges unexpectedly from the shadows, crosses the street and then disappears again into the darkness.

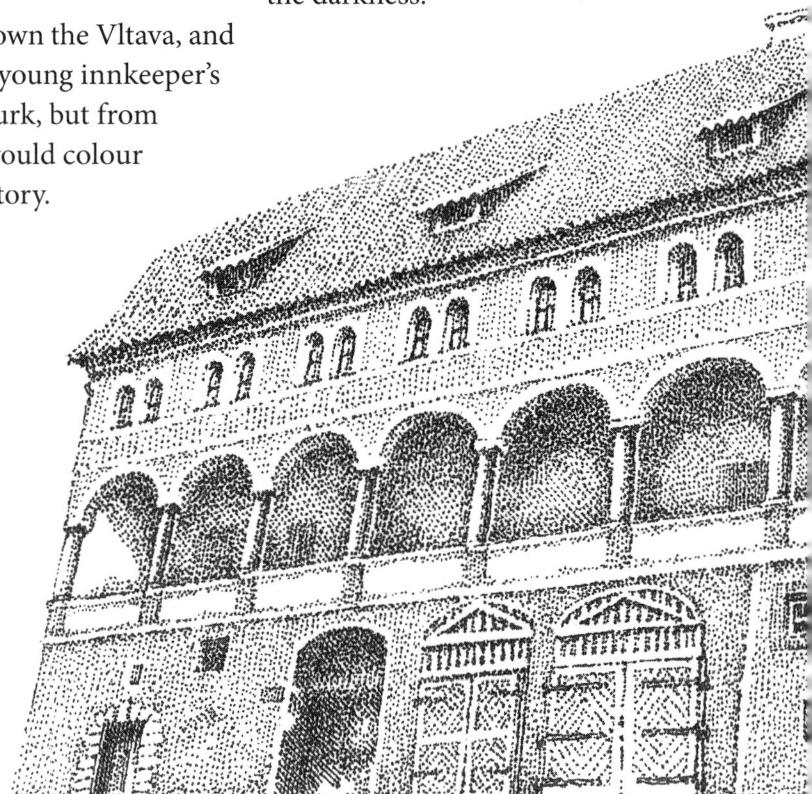

The Jewish Town

THE OLD, NEW SYNAGOGUE

In the beginning a small wooden prayer room stood in the middle of the Jewish Town, but over time, as the population increased, only a few families could fit inside. A new and bigger synagogue needed to be built, but even the oldest and most respected elders could not agree where to build it. In the end they were helped by happenstance.

Once, while playing on a hill covered in bushes and grass, some children came across a regular row of hewn stones. They ran to tell their parents about the discovery and the parents agreed that the place for the new synagogue had in fact been chosen.

They excavated the hill, carted away the dirt, and in the end they uncovered a whole contiguous wall. Then they recalled the ancient story that angels had once brought rare stones from the ruins of the Temple of Jerusalem to the banks of the Vltava, in fact a whole synagogue, which had been hidden in the hill.

The wise elders decided: "Use the stones to build a new synagogue. It should be as similar as possible to the Temple of Jerusalem. The window openings should narrow toward the inside, the mighty vault should rest on two pillars, and the believers should descend into the temple down nine steps!"

A new synagogue was built on the old stone foundations and thus it received the name "Old-New".

"When the Temple of Jerusalem is to be built again, the hewn stones must be returned – that was the angels' condition," the elders believed.

Out of respect for the structure's sacred origin, subsequent generations never dared to change anything on its walls. They became dark under layers of dust and dirt, coated with all the good and evil that history brought, withstanding fires, and the synagogue has thus retained its original form to this day.

THE GOLEM

Create a creature of clay that will help you against all your enemies! – This strange counsel appeared in a dream to a Jewish scholar from Prague, a rabbi by the name of Jehuda Löw ben Bezalel. It was likely because the Jews had once again become the target of hate-driven attacks and the rabbi no longer knew how to protect his people.

The next day he headed to the banks of the Vltava with two helpers, found a place with fine moist clay and formed it into an enormous man – a golem. Just before he finished the rabbi inserted a roll of parchment, containing an arcane inscription, into its mouth. At that moment the figure shook, opened its eyes and rose – it was gigantic.

"We should dress him the way servants in the synagogue dress," the rabbi decided, and led the dressed golem home. He explained to his wife:

"This is a new servant, his name is Josef. He will help out in the synagogue and sleep at our place, but do not use him for everyday housework."

The rabbi's wife promised her husband that she would abide by his words, but once, when she had so much work that she didn't know up from down and she kept passing by the inert golem, she could bear it no longer and asked him to carry water to the tub. She herself ran off to town to run an errand. When she returned shortly she could see from far off how people were gathered around her home and water was pouring out of the door.

"Josef, that's enough," she called to the golem and calmed down the neighbours.

From then on she took care not to ask the golem for even the smallest services that did not relate to holy work in the temple.

During the day the golem helped the rabbi out in the synagogue, and in the evening he walked the streets of the ghetto keeping watch. Most of the time he did not even need to do anything, because his size evoked fear in everyone, even those with malicious intentions.

The golem saved the ghetto from pillaging and the killing of innocents many times. He was a good man, working all week without tiring. Quite the opposite, in fact: at the end of the week it seemed that he had more and more energy. The rabbi began to worry that the golem's strength could grow to such an extent that instead of helping he would begin to destroy things, so on the Sabbath he put a different scroll in the golem's mouth, one for calm and rest.

It once happened that the rabbi's young daughter fell ill. The rabbi was so taxed thinking about her that as the Sabbath approached he completely forgot about the golem.

And the golem's strength grew. By evening he could no longer sit still, pacing back and forth around the room. Then he went out into the street and began breaking windows and doors, ripping trees out of the ground, tearing down iron signboards with frightening ease. He returned to the rabbi's home like a storm and began throwing furniture out of the window, smashing dishes, tearing down paintings and statues, raging like a beast.

The noise of the tumult reached the synagogue. When the rabbi's frightened maid ran to him and told him of the havoc being wreaked, the rabbi stopped the prayers and ran out into the street:

"Josef, enough, that's enough," he said, calming the golem. Then he approached him and changed the scrolls in his mouth. "Josef, go home and rest."

The rabbi returned to the synagogue and finished the prayers. The Song for the Sabbath, which announces the arrival of the Sabbath, was sung again from the start, and since then, in memory of this event, the Old New Synagogue is the only synagogue in the world where the ninety-second psalm is always sung twice.

Once he returned home, Rabbi Löw said to the golem:

"Josef, go to the temple attic, lie down there and rest." Josef obeyed, went up to the attic, lay down in the dust, closed his eyes and fell asleep. The rabbi came to him and withdrew the arcane scroll from his mouth. He burned the golem's work clothes and covered the body with the remnants of old clothes.

"The golem left in the night and won't return," he told everyone and, just in case, he issued an order that no one was to enter the attic of the Old New Synagogue. He was afraid that someone might try to reanimate the golem. And his fear was justified.

Time passed, and once a poor wandering student appeared in Prague's Jewish Town. He had read somewhere about an artificial man, about the golem, and he said to himself that he must find this man to help him out of poverty – the golem could bring him as much money as he needed, the finest delicacies, the most expensive jewellery. That was how the student imagined it. He studied many books, read many rare scrolls and he wrote on a piece of parchment what he thought would animate the golem. At dusk he set out for the attic of the Old New Synagogue.

In the weak light of a candle he searched the attic, but found only layers of dust and cobwebs. Then in the corner he discovered a pile of half-decomposed rags. He began to toss them aside, and under the last layer he found a layer of clay formed into a figure. He realised he had found what he was searching for. He pulled his scrap of parchment out of his pocket and placed it in the golem's mouth.

At first, nothing happened. Suddenly, just when the student thought that he had made a mistake, the golem shook and his chest began to rise and fall. He was breathing. Then he sat up and slowly rose. He staggered, shook as if in a fever, and began to grow. He grew and grew, reaching to the rafters.

The student realised he must have made a fatal error in his formula. He scrambled up into the rafters and quickly withdrew the scroll from the golem's mouth. The golem shook, quivered and then collapsed to the floor. As he fell, he landed on the student, burying him under a pile of clay.

The legend of the golem haunted many scholars and researchers, but those that were allowed into the attic of the Old New Synagogue never found the golem's remains.

THE JEWISH CEMETERY

Prague was hit by the plague and the streets of the Jewish Town were not spared. It did not pick and choose its victims – young and old died, rich and poor, but what was worst of all, many small children were dying. The rabbi was very upset and worried that soon all the ghetto's inhabitants would die. He pored over wise books long into the night and thought about how to drive away the angel of death, which was stretching its wings over the ghetto and indeed all of Prague.

One night the rabbi had a strange dream about fresh graves where the small children who had died in recent days lay under the dirt. The rabbi stood among the gravestones, when suddenly the graves began to open and the children began crawling out of them. They swarmed around the cemetery, running, jumping, playing and dancing. The rabbi watched them in his dream and didn't know what it was supposed to mean. When the features of the gravestones and children began to break up, he awoke.

In the morning he called his most faithful servant to him:

"Of all my students you are the bravest and most courageous, this is why I am asking you for help," Rabbi Löw said to him. "I'm not sure why the angel of death refuses to leave us, but the only hope is that the children, as innocent beings, will tell us. At midnight you will go to the graveyard and wait until the graves open and the children climb out of them. Hide behind a tombstone until one of the children comes close. Then take his shroud and quickly run with it to me."

"Yes, my teacher, I shall do all that you have asked of me," the pupil promised.

Indeed, the student undertook his task without fear. An hour after midnight he returned to the rabbi with a white shroud that he had torn off a playing black-haired boy.

Both rabbi and student sat by the window and waited to see what would happen. The clock struck one and a black-haired boy appeared, ran straight to the rabbi's home and tapped on the window.

"Please give me back my shroud. Without it I cannot return underground. And the children won't play with me, I'm sad. Please," the boy implored.

"I don't want you to be unhappy, boy, but nor do I want any more parents to be unhappy worrying about their children. I will return your shroud, but first tell me, why so many children are dying all over? Why them in particular?" the rabbi inquired.

The boy cried and continued to beg for his shroud back. The rabbi held firm, though with great pity.

"Two women live nearby here and they summoned the angel of death because they had killed a newborn."

The rabbi returned the shroud to the boy and the very next morning he called upon the two women. It did not take long before they confessed and even testified before the court.

The judgment was strict, but immediately after that the angel of death left the Jewish Town and the plague subsided.

Thus Rabbi Löw saved not only many children from the Jewish Town, but also many inhabitants of all Prague from the Black Death.

THE GOLD COINS IN A CLOTH AND MAISEL'S SYNAGOGUE

Once, Rabbi Yitzhak – a respected and wealthy man – was returning from his travels. It was already pitch dark when his carriage set out into the forest among the trees. They couldn't see a thing.

After a while a light appeared in front of them. The rabbi had his carriage stop and got out to follow the light to the edge of a clearing. The sight he saw took his breath away: two elves were running to and fro by a large pile of gold. They were gathering gold into pouches and carrying it off into the brush.

The rabbi turned to the elves to find out who such riches belonged to.

"A man from the Jewish Town. But it's not you," the elf snapped.

"And when will he receive all these riches?" asked the rabbi, refusing to be dismissed.

The elf grinned: "Once your daughter is wed."

"Can I take at least three gold coins as a souvenir?" the rabbi asked.

"You may not, we would be short. But you can trade: take three from the treasure and leave us three of yours."

The rabbi gave the elf three gold pieces and took three from the pile. At that moment the elves and the treasure disappeared.

For the rest of the journey to Prague the rabbi thought about how to resolve the riddle. He had an idea: if he placed one of the gold coins on the street, it must only be picked up by the one for whom the whole treasure was intended.

The next day he wrapped a gold coin in a cloth, threw it out of his window onto the street, and waited. The whole day nothing happened; no one noticed the cloth until the evening, when a grubby little boy appeared in the street, picked up the cloth, and disappeared with it around the next corner.

This was a surprise for the rabbi. This street urchin was supposed to be the rich man? Unsatisfied, the rabbi wrapped another gold coin in a rag and again the ragged boy carried it off. The third day the same thing happened again. The rabbi was vexed. He released an announcement that he had lost three gold coins and whoever found them should return them to him. Hardly a moment passed and the little boy came to the rabbi:

"Excuse me, sir, I didn't know they belonged to you. Three nights in a row

I dreamt that I would find a gold coin wrapped in a rag in front of your house. And it was true. Don't be angry, sir, but I can only return two. The third I gave to my mother, who needed it. Once she sells her goods I will return it to you."

The rabbi was pleased by the boy's honesty and was convinced that he had found the future owner of the golden treasure. He found out that the boy's name was Mordechai, that he was the son of the half-blind porter Maisel, and that he was from a very poor but respectable family.

"I have become fond of your son Mordechai. He is clever and honest. I want to take care of him as if he were my own and give him an education," the rabbi said to Mordechai's father.

The father was grudging, not wanting to give up his last son, but when the rabbi promised to give Mordechai his daughter, he gave his consent.

Everything happened according to the rabbi's wish: Mordechai studied diligently, became close to the rabbi's daughter and in time he took her as his wife.

But lo! No treasure appeared under the rabbi's roof.

The rabbi turned all his frustration and then ill-will against Mordechai and his hatred deepened so much that his son-in-law and his wife, the rabbi's daughter, had to move out.

But Mordechai lived an honest life and was successful in his business, and the couple were content.

After a year or so a man came into his shop wanting to buy some goods. Mordechai offered him only the best and the man chose what he wanted.

"I don't have enough money," the man admitted. "Could I pay you with an old wrought chest for now?"

Mordechai agreed. Several days later the man kept his word and brought him the chest. He unloaded it with the coachman at the shop and hurried away.

Mordechai examined the chest and its rusted lock. As soon as he touched it, the lid opened of its own accord and the room was bathed in the light emanating from a mountain of gold and silver inside.

Mordechai Maisel became a wealthy man, but he used the money for the benefit of the whole ghetto: he had two synagogues built, one of them bearing his name – the Maisel Synagogue. He also had women's baths built, founded an orphanage, an almshouse and a hospital, had the muddy streets paved and took care of the dowry for many poor brides.

After Mordechai's death, as so often happens, the rest of his wealth became the cause of many property disputes, court battles and bad blood.

St Agnes Convent

THE MIRACULOUS SWALLOW WATER

Once, an impoverished Polish noblewoman took shelter at the St Agnes Convent. The nuns took her in, took care of her because she was sick, and in general took pity on her. The woman was touched by their care, saying:

"I would like to repay you for your care, but I have no gold or money. But I will share with you my family's ancient secret – a recipe for preparing miraculous water, a healing medicine. It is called swallow water."

From that time the nuns prepared the miracle cure precisely according to the recipe and gave it away or sold it for a token amount to the needy. People thus began to travel to the convent from near and far.

However, time is without mercy. The noblewoman died, the convent was closed and there was danger that the secret of the miraculous swallow water would be forgotten forever. Luckily, one of the nuns decided that she would save the secret, continuing to prepare the elixir and give it away for free around the convent. She kept her promise, but even she could not fight time. She grew old, and when she departed from this world she took the secret of the miraculous water with her. All that she left behind were the few remaining bottles, which the landlady, at whose home the nun lived, squirreled away as her greatest treasure.

As it happened, a few years later, a young student from Poland rented a room with her. He said that he came from the same family as the noblewoman who had died at the convent.

"I am of the same clan and it was our custom only to pass on the ancient recipe on our deathbed," he confessed. "And unfortunately the only person who knew the secret died here at the convent. As the family tradition has been disrupted, I am trying to determine the content of the swallow water through various experiments."

The landlady eventually agreed and brought the student one of the last bottles of elixir and told him everything she knew about its preparation.

The student tried everything possible and impossible to find out what the swallow water was made from. He spent long nights conducting his experiments, until some began to suspect him of black magic.

This was likely the reason why one curious watchman climbed up to the student's window just before dawn to see if there was any truth in the rumours. Just when he reached the level of the window and was leaning forward anxiously to see into the room, a deafening explosion rang out and smoke and colourful flames poured out of the window. The explosion threw the watchman down onto the cobblestones and woke all the people in the surrounding streets. Within minutes a curious mob had gathered in front of the house. Some of them quickly entered the student's room, where they found only remnants of wood from the furniture, shattered glass and in the middle of the devastation the student's scorched body.

That was truly the end of the secret of the swallow water, the healing elixir that had brought so many people relief from pain and suffering.

Carolinum

THE BRIDAL VEIL

As we all know, luck is fickle. This was once experienced by a rich Prague burgher named Rotlev.

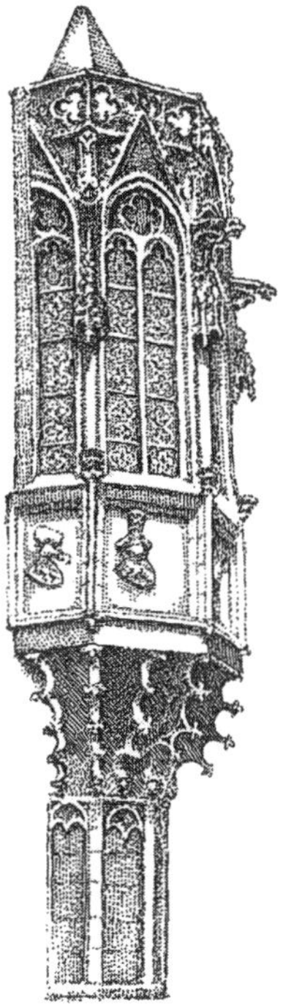

All at once he lost his homes, his gardens and vineyards, and he grew poorer and poorer. But as he was not used to just giving up, he fixated on a gold mine in Jílové u Prahy.

He acquired mining rights and it seemed the vein of gold he hit upon right away would bring him luck. But he was wrong. The gold vein petered out, Rotlev didn't have enough to pay his miners, and he had no peace at home either. He was so obsessed with the vein of gold that he didn't eat or sleep and he hardly said a word to his wife and children. He lived as if in a fever, paid out the last of his money and then he began to borrow, living on credit.

"Give up digging already," everyone told him, "while there's still time." But their advice fell on deaf ears. In the end Rotlev remained completely alone in the mine. He dug and dug until he collapsed with fatigue, but without success.

One day, when saddling his horse on the way to the mine and somewhat suspecting it would be his last journey, his wife came to him.

"For luck, my dear," she said, handing him a gold-laced wedding veil, a memento of their happy times. "Sell it, it's the last valuable thing we have."

"Thank you, my dear," Rotlev responded, tears in his eyes. "It will not be easy, but maybe it will truly bring us luck."

Rotlev made a good sale of the veil and could buy new tools to continue digging. He hammered into the rock with all his strength and suddenly hit upon a vein of gold. At first he didn't believe that the vein wouldn't fade again, but when it continued to grow stronger he knew that luck had smiled upon him again.

At last he could pay off all his debts. With the first money he made he bought his wife a new richly embroidered veil, expanded his mine and repaired his home.

After Rotlev's death his house was acquired by Prague University and they named it after Emperor Charles IV. It belongs to them to this day.

Wenceslas Square

A PRAYER TO SAINT WENCESLAS

In the seventeenth century, Bohemia was hit by a great crop failure and famine. Prague was the worst off. The New Town aldermen consulted for a long time until they agreed that they would ask the emperor himself for assistance. Only one alderman, the oldest, disagreed:

"I don't like the fact that you have forgotten your most powerful allies. If they do not take care of us, things will be bad. I'm not saying don't buy grain from abroad, I'm only saying do not expect anything for free."

"What allies do you mean? How have we forgotten them?" the portreeve asked in wonder.

"You do not know who our greatest allies are? They are our Czech patron saints. Our forefathers appealed to them when times were hard, particularly to Saint Wenceslas. But you do not," the oldest councillor said with reproach. "You would rather take your appeal to foreigners than seek the help of those who have never abandoned us."

The portreeve agreed: "You are right. Let us go to the church and ask the Czech patron saints for help."

The priest had barely concluded his prayer when the sky clouded over and rain began to fall. It rained for so long that the drought-stricken ground sopped up the water and the grain began to grow and gave such a harvest as the people could hardly remember.

The famine and misery ended, and the aldermen ruled that they would have a sculpture carved in thanks to Saint Wenceslas. They placed it at the top of Wenceslas Square (formerly the Horse Market), where it stood until 1879.

It is said that the statue has special power. When the final battle takes place between the Czechs and their enemies on Wenceslas Square, and a single drop of blood touches the statue of Prince Wenceslas, he will come to life, raise his spear, and wave his sword toward Blaník Mountain. The mountain will open up, the Knights of Blaník will pour out toward Prague and forever banish our foes. Only then will a time of peace and prosperity rule in Bohemia.

Karlova Street

THE FIERY SKELETON

Once, a fire broke out on Karlova Street. It was right next to the house of an greedy old moneylender. The fire spread quickly through the street. People carried old people, children and furniture out of their burning homes and tried to put it out, helping one another.

When the flames were hungrily climbing higher and higher into the sky, the old moneylender ran out of his home with a sack over his shoulder and fled toward the Vltava.

"Don't leave, return and help us carry water," his neighbours called to him, "every body counts!"

But the moneylender didn't turn around, holding tightly to his sack full of money and hurrying away from the tragedy.

After a time, when the smoke had dispersed and life on Karlova Street had returned to normal, the moneylender's house remained empty. No one knew what had actually happened to him; it was as if the ground had swallowed him up.

Until one night, when he appeared, bent low, dragging the heavy sack, his knees buckling.

"Help, help me," he beseeched the passersby, "just a little bit, at least a few steps."

Those who knew him avoided him, and those who took pity on him and drew near to help him fled in fear. Before their eyes he transformed into a fiery skeleton: the flames burned from his eye sockets and his bones glowed like rusty embers.

Whenever the fiery skeleton appeared on Karlova Street it usually foretold some great misfortune – a fire or flood.

Were anyone daring enough to help the fiery man carry his burden from Charles Bridge along Karlova Street to the Old Town Square, the moneylender would be rid of his curse. But so far everyone has turned away from him and fled as fast and as far as possible.

THE MAD BARBER

Once, a long time ago, under the rule of Rudolph II, a barber opened a business. He did well and did not suffer from poverty, but he was not happy. He wanted more property. To accumulate, multiply, simply magnify his wealth to infinite proportions.

His unbridled desire for wealth took over his whole being. Producing gold, piles of gold, was his only goal, and so he dedicated himself to the rituals of magical alchemy.

He had a wife and three daughters. At first they interpreted his appetite for magic as a passing phase, but when the family's savings began to slip away in purchases of special retorts, flasks, potions and other arcane odds and ends, they warned him:

"You will destroy us, father, if you don't stop spending our only savings. Return to your honest trade as a barber, father, don't become charmed by false visions of gold," his daughters cautioned.

"Nothing good will come of it," his wife added.

And she was right. In the end greed destroyed the man and his whole family. Nothing remained of the money the family had stored away for hard times.

They had to sell their home, the daughters began to support themselves with prostitution and his wife could not bear their hor rible fate. She decided to end her miserable life and one day she jumped from a high wall. The barber then went utterly mad. He did not have enough for a crust of bread; all that remained was his barber's razor. In a daze he wandered the streets, attacking passers-by, waving his razor around, Once, he fell upon on a group of soldiers and it did not turn out well. The soldiers were strong and there were enough of them to defend themselves. The barber did not survive his wounds.

Today the ghost of the mad barber still wanders Karlova Street looking for a brave soul that will let him give them a shave and thereby free him.

Clementinum

THE SECRET CACHE

In the 16th century, Jesuits took up residence in the Clementinum in Prague and founded a monastery and schools there. When Pope Clement XIV disbanded the Jesuit Order, they had to move. They had experienced this before, so they believed they would return to the Clementinum. Together they agreed that they would hide their precious gems, gold and silver in a secret hiding place.

A poor bricklayer lived on the banks of the Vltava in a small house. One evening two cloaked men knocked on his door. "We come in peace," they assured him. "We have work for you and we will reward you generously for it."

As the bricklayer did not have much money, he did not think long, though the mysterious men worried him, and he agreed. The men asked him to take his tools and follow them. Then they added: "The work is secret, no one may learn of it. If you say a single word to anyone, ill will befall you."

The bricklayer agreed and sat with them in the carriage they had prepared. The men blindfolded him, and the carriage set out. The bricklayer thought he could count the corners every time the carriage turned so he would know where they were going, but he was wrong. The carriage switched streets and rode in circles until the bricklayer was completely disoriented.

At long last they stopped. The men helped the bricklayer out of the carriage and led him along a long corridor. They went down and then up a narrow staircase until they suddenly stopped and one of the men took off the blindfold. His eyes quickly adjusted to the dim light and he could make out a small cellar, with bricks and mortar prepared by the wall. The men showed him a small opening to the neighbouring cellar and instructed him to wall it up. The bricklayer asked nothing of them and set to work. He only managed to notice large and small wrought crates stacked on top of each other in the adjacent cellar.

When he had finished he received a rich reward, then they covered his eyes again and took him home by a circuitous route to his cottage by the river.

"We remind you, you must never mention these matters to anyone, otherwise you will come to a bad end," the men repeated to him in parting and quickly departed.

After a time, rumours spread around Prague that the Jesuits had not surrendered all their property and that they must have hidden the majority of their treasures. And so it seemed to the bricklayer that his secret work might have had something to do with this.

He went to the town hall, where he told them everything in great detail. They set out with him to the Clementinum at once and examined all the walls, ceilings and floors in the cellar, but found nothing.

And so the bricklayer believed until his death that the treasure lay walled up somewhere in the cellar of the Clementinum.

Vyšehrad

WISE LIBUŠE

Princess Libuše was a wise and just woman, resolute and kind to her people. She could also foresee the future. The people held her in great esteem.

Once she had to judge a quarrel between two men who could not agree on the boundary between their fields. They argued and argued, each explaining the injustice as they saw it. She listened to them silently and then passed her fair judgment. But the man who had lost could not bear his failure. He became angry and cried:

"Shame on men who are ruled by a woman! We all know that women have long hair but are short on sense. It is a disgrace that we do not have a man to govern us and that we allow ourselves to be ruled by women without dissent."

The man's words deeply wounded Libuše, but she restrained herself and replied graciously:

"Yes, I am a woman, and for this reason I rule as a woman. And you do not heed my words, you live without fear and shame, and so you must have a governor who is crueler than a woman. Now go home and come back tomorrow."

The next day all the people and elders of the clan met and Princess Libuše spoke to those assembled:

"People, I feel sorry for you. You do not know how to appreciate your freedom and you would rather bow your head before a man you have elected and who rules you with a strong hand. I don't want to frighten you, but I will tell you what the gods have shown me. Therefore, choose your duke wisely, for it is easy to install a ruler, but hard to unseat one."

The people rejoiced and everyone asked her to tell them who they should look for.

Libuše stood, raised her hand and proclaimed:

"Lo, beyond the mountains by the river Bílina a village called Stadice stretches out. There your prince is ploughing his field with two mottled oxen. His name is Přemysl and he is the man whose descendants will rule this country through the ages."

The designated emissaries set out to find Přemysl, following the princess's horse. They gave the ploughman her message and asked him to return with them to Vyšehrad.

The ploughman changed into princely robes, sat upon the horse and took his polished bast shoes with him.

They set out together.

One of the emissaries found courage and asked the future prince why he had taken the shoes he wore in the field with him.

"I shall keep them so that our descendants will know from whence they came. So that they will live honestly without oppressing anyone, as we are all equal by nature."

When the delegation drew close to Vyšehrad, the princess met them with her entourage and a crowd of curious people. They all welcomed the new prince with joy and led him to the prince's stone seat.

Then they celebrated, ate and drank, sang and played. They celebrated long into the night and in the morning light Vyšehrad was still ringing with their joyous merriment.

HORYMÍR AND BRAVE ŠEMÍK

During the reign of Prince Křesomysl, silver was extensively mined in Bohemia and people left the countryside to dig, leaving their fields fallow. And so there was plenty of silver, but little bread. Many squires and yeomen warned the prince that he should hold bread in higher esteem than gold and silver, but Křesomysl, dazzled by the lustre of the precious metal, would not heed their advice.

Of all the lesser nobility, it was Horymír, a bold and wise man, who was worried the most by the prince's negligence.

"More than gold and silver the people need bread," he declared, and asked the prince to revoke the mining rights.

Most of all it was the miners who did not like his words, and they conspired to punish Horymír. Like a wild pack of dogs they hurried to Horymír's fortress. He did not wait for them, however, he mounted his faithful steed Šemík and saved himself from being overwhelmed.

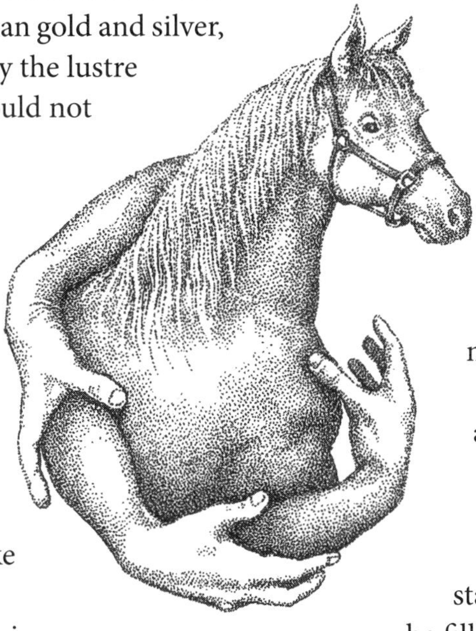

In a rage that Horymír had eluded them, the miners scattered his grain stores and burned them.

"Horymír is afraid of hunger, so let him taste it himself," some of them called.

"Let them cut me with my own sword if I do not repay them for this!" Horymír swore at the red glow on the horizon emanating from the land near his home.

As soon as the miners had left, Horymír gathered all his people and set out towards the mining pits of Příbram. In the dim light of dusk he and his closest friends fell upon the miners' houses, burning them down, and whoever resisted was stabbed with a sword. Then he filled in the mines with rock and dirt.

That same night, Horymír appeared at Vyšehrad, but told the prince nothing of what had happened.

It did not take long though: at dawn, the miners came to complain to the prince.

Křesomysl had Horymír summoned and asked him why he had damaged him so. Horymír denied everything and explained nothing, so the prince had him thrown in jail, from whence he would see the light of day only at his trial before the elders and squires.

The crowd of miners demanded Horymír's death by immolation, and because the voice of the miners was everything to Křesomysl, he sentenced Horymir to death, not by burning at the pyre, but by the "gentler" method of beheading.

"Noble prince, permit me as one sentenced to death to take a ride on my faithful Šemík, and then you can do with me what you wish," Horymír said.

The prince laughed at this odd wish, but he ordered all the gates to be closed and in a mocking voice said:

"Have a ride, but Šemík does not have wings, he cannot help you."

Horymír led Šemík out of the stable, saddled him, spoke quietly with him for a moment, and then swung up into the saddle. Everyone in the courtyard admired the beautiful, lush horse. His legs danced, he turned in a circle, and when Horymír whooped, Šemík reared and went round the courtyard for the first time with long, light leaps.

Horymír whooped again and Šemík crossed the courtyard from one gate to the next in one long, gliding leap.

By the castle walls Horymír whooped for a third time and shouted:

"Šemík, up!"

The horse responded with a human voice: "Sir, hold on!"

He reared up and with a colossal leap rose over the walls and disappeared from sight.

Everyone froze in horror. They ran to the walls expecting to see the horse and rider dashed upon the rocks below, but there they froze in amazement again. Šemík and Horymír were speeding away at a gallop through the valley.

This unprecedented act softened the heart of the prince and he pardoned Horymír. But Horymír could not rejoice, because his beloved Šemík had hurt himself badly jumping from the rock.

Horymír rushed back to the fortress and went right to Šemík.

"My Lord," Šemík spoke with a human voice, "I know I am not long for this world. Do not throw my body to the birds or beasts of prey, but bury me before the gates of the fortress."

And so it was. Horymír buried Šemík before the gates of the fortress and placed a large stone there as a tombstone, which to this day shows where his faithful Šemík was buried.

U Prašného mostu
Mariánské hradby
Jelení
Chotkova
Na Opyši
Staré zám. schody
U Brusnice
Prague Castle
Valdštejnská
Klárov
U Kasáren
Hradčanské nám.
Valdštejnské nám.
Letenská
Zám. schody
Ke hradu
Loreta Square
Nerudova
Malostranské nám.
U Lužického semináře
Cihelna
Úvoz
Jánský vršek
Mostecká
nám. Dražického
Vlašská
Vlašská
Tržiště
Karmelitská
Strahov Monastery
Charles
Velkopřevor. nám.
Maltézské nám.
Nebovidská
Nosticova
The Church of Our Lady of Victory
U Sovových mlýnů
Újezd
Všehrdova
Malostr. náb.
Strahovská
Říční
Olympijská
most
Vítězná
Újezd
Plaská
Chaloupeckého
Janáčkovo nábřeží
Zborovská
Mělnická
Šermířská
Jezdecká
Petřínská
El. Peškové
Holečkova
Vodní

nábřeží Edvarda Beneše
Čechův most
Štefánikův most
nábř. Ludvíka Svobody
ovo nábřeží
St Agnes Convent
Dušní
Hradební
Revoluční
Haštalské nám.
Elišky Krásnohorské
Bílkova
Soukenická
Věžeňská
Haštalská
Pařížská
Kozí
Dlouhá
Truhlářská
The Jewish Town
sův most
nám. Jana Palacha
Široká
Masná
Na Poříčí
Kaprova
nám. Republiky
Clementinum
Old Town Square
Ungelt
Celetná
Hybernská
Linhartská
Malé nám.
Senovážná
Ovocný trh
Karlova Street
Carolinum
Na Příkopě
Senovážné nám.
Anenská
Nekázanka
Havelská
V Kotcích
Rytířská
Na Můstku
Panská
Náprstkova
Betlémské nám.
Betlémská
28. října
Konviktská
Karoliny Světlé
Na Perštýně
Jindřišská
Růžová
Smetanovo náb.
Bartolomějská
Politických vězňů
Wenceslas Square
Divadelní
Národní
Jungmannova
Purkyňova
Vodičkova
Ostrovní
Spálená
Vladislavova
V Jámě
Štěpánská
Školská
Lazarská
Ve Smečkách
Krakovská
Mezibranská
30 min.
Vyšehrad
Navrátilova
Myslíkova
Řeznická

CONTENTS

PRAGUE 5

PRAGUE CASTLE
- Žito the Magician 7
- Dalibor and Daliborka 9
- Paleček the Jester 10

THE CATHEDRAL OF ST VITUS, ST WENCESLAS AND ST ADALBERT
- The St Vitus Bells 13
- The Zikmund Bell and the Rope of Human Hair 14
- The Miraculous Helm of Prince Wenceslas 15

STRAHOV MONASTERY
- The Pious Abbot 17
- The Skeleton's Justice 18

LORETA SQUARE
- Signature from Beyond the Grave 21
- Bread Crust Slippers 22
- The Singing Loreta Bells 24

CHARLES BRIDGE
- Parler's Recipe 27
- Perun's Sword 28
- Prince Bruncvík and the Magic Sword 28
- The Devil's Ruse 30
- Two Dreams and One Treasure 33
- Punished Pride 34
- King Wenceslas and Brave Zuzana 35

THE CHURCH OF OUR LADY OF VICTORY
- The Infant Jesus of Prague 37

THE OLD TOWN ASTRONOMICAL CLOCK
- Master Hanuš 41
- The Skeleton's Power 42
- The Prisoner and the Sparrow 43

OLD TOWN SQUARE
The Twenty-Seven Executed 45
The Immured Child 46

UNGELT
The Smitten Turk 49

THE JEWISH TOWN
The Old, New Synagogue 53
The Golem 54
The Jewish Cemetery 56
The Gold Coins in a Cloth and Maisel's Synagogue 58

ST AGNES CONVENT
The Miraculous Swallow Water 61

CAROLINUM
The Bridal Veil 65

WENCESLAS SQUARE
A Prayer to Saint Wenceslas 67

KARLOVA STREET
The Fiery Skeleton 69
The Mad Barber 70

CLEMENTINUM
The Secret Cache 73

VYŠEHRAD
Wise Libuše 77
Horymír and Brave Šemík 79

The following publications were drawn upon for this literary treatment: Cibula, V.: *Pražské pověsti.* Panorama, Prague 1983; Jirásek, A.: *Staré pověsti české.* Albatros, Prague 2003; Košnář, J.: *Staropražské pověsti a legendy.* Odeon, Prague 1992; Meyrink, G.: *Golem.* Topič, Prague 1917; Tomek, V. V.: *Pražské židovské pověsti a legendy.* Volvox Globator, Prague 2007; Wenig, A.: *Staré pověsti pražské.* Omega, Prague 2013.

Prague in Legends

Illustrated by Jan Klimeš.
Compiled and written by Anna Novotná.
Graphic design and cover by Jan Klimeš.
Typesetting by Hana Klimešová.
Printed by Tiskárny Havlíčkův Brod, a. s.
Published by Práh, Patočkova 2386/85, 169 00 Prague 6, www.prah.cz,
in 2016 as its 595th publication.

First edition.